Book Belongs To

In this book you will learn about list of verbs there meanings, past tense, presesnt tense, future tense, Imperative & Infinitive from verbs. So let's Jump.

Verbs are one of the most important components of a sentence as they indicate the action or state of being performed by the subject. They play a crucial role in conveying the meaning and adding dynamic energy to writing. In this book, we will explore various types of verbs, their tenses, and how they can be effectively used to enhance the narrative and engage the reader. Whether you are a beginner or an experienced writer, this guide will provide you with a comprehensive understanding of the power of verbs and help you become a more confident and skilled writer.
As we added cursive style you can learn the verbs & practice cursive handwriting at same time.

VERB

A verb is a word that expresses an action, occurrence, or state of being. Verbs are one of the most important components of a sentence as they convey the main idea and provide information about the subject. Verbs can be used in different tenses to indicate the time frame in which the action or state of being is occurring. For example, the verb "run" can be used in the present tense (I run), the past tense (I ran), and the future tense (I will run). Verbs can also be used in different forms to express the mood of the sentence, such as the imperative mood (Run!) or the infinitive form (to run). Understanding verbs and their various forms and functions is an essential component of effective writing, as they provide the energy and momentum that drives the narrative forward.

PAST TENSE

Past tense is a grammatical category used to describe actions, events, or states that have already happened. It is a way of expressing events in a chronological order and creates a sense of past time in writing. In English, past tense is indicated by various verb forms such as "-ed" for regular verbs and irregular verb forms such as "went" for the verb "go." The use of past tense allows writers to recount past events, describe past states or conditions, and create a sense of nostalgia or reminiscence. This grammatical category is an essential tool for writers, as it enables them to craft narratives that are rich in detail and full of depth and meaning. Whether you are writing fiction or non-fiction, an understanding of past tense is crucial for effective storytelling. In this book, we will explore the various forms of past tense and how to use them to bring your writing to life.

Example:

1. I verb (past)
2. you verb (past)
3. he/she/it verb (past)
4. we verb (past)
5. you verb (past)
6. they verb (past)

For the Past Perfect you add "had" after the pronouns

1. I had verb (past form)
2. you had verb (past form)
3. he/she/it had verb (past form)
4. we had verb (past form)
5. you had verb (past form)
6. they had verb (past form)

For Past Prefect Continous you add "had been" after the pronouns

1. I had been Verb -ing form
2. you had been Verb -ing form
3. he/she/it had been Verb -ing form
4. we had been Verb -ing form
5. you had been Verb -ing form
6. they had been Verb -ing form

PRESENT TENSE

Present tense refers to a grammatical category used to describe actions, events, or states that are happening now. It is a way of expressing events as they occur in real-time and creates a sense of immediacy in writing. In English, present tense is indicated by various verb forms such as "run" for the verb "run." The use of present tense allows writers to describe events as they unfold, express feelings and thoughts in the moment, and create a sense of immediacy and urgency. Present tense is a versatile tool for writers and is commonly used in a variety of genres, including fiction, non-fiction, and poetry.

Present Contionus

1. I am Verb -ing form
2. You are Verb -ing form
3. He/she/it is Verb -ing form
4. We are Verb -ing form
5. You are Verb -ing form
6. They are Verb -ing form

Present Perfect Contionus

1. I have been Verb -ing form
2. you have been Verb -ing form
3. he/she/it has been Verb -ing form
4. we have been Verb -ing form
5. you have been Verb -ing form
6. they have been Verb -ing form

Present Perfect

1. I have Verb
2. you have Verb
3. he/she/it has Verb
4. we have Verb
5. you have Verb
6. they have Verb

FUTURE TENSE

Future tense refers to a grammatical category used to describe actions, events, or states that will take place in the future. It is a way of expressing events that have not yet happened and creates a sense of anticipation in writing. In English, future tense is often indicated by using auxiliary verbs such as "will" or "shall" in combination with the base form of the verb, such as "will run." The

or "shall" in combination with the base form of the verb, such as "will run." The use of future tense allows writers to describe future events and plans, express predictions and expectations, and create a sense of hope or uncertainty. Future tense is an important tool for writers and is often used to add depth and dimension to narratives, build suspense, and shape the reader's expectations.

1. I will Verb
2. you will Verb
3. he/she/it will Verb
4. we will Verb
5. you will Verb
6. they will Verb

Future Perfect

1. I will have Verb
2. you will have Verb
3. he/she/it will have Verb
4. we will have Ver
5. byou will have Verb
6. they will have Verb

Future Prefect contiouns

1. I will have been Verb -ing form
2. you will have been Verb -ing form
3. he/she/it will have been Verb -ing form
4. we will have been Verb -ing form
5. you will have been Verb -ing form
6. they will have been Verb -ing form

IMPERATIVE

Imperative is a grammatical mood used to express commands, requests, or advice. It is a way of giving orders or making requests in a direct and forceful manner. In English, the imperative mood is often indicated by using the base form of the verb, such as "run." The use of the imperative mood is common in situations where the speaker is giving orders or making requests, such as in instructions, recipes, or persuasive writing. Imperative sentences typically have an implied subject, which is understood to be "you." The use of the imperative mood can make writing more direct and powerful, and is an important tool for writers who want to create a sense of urgency or encourage action.

INFNITIVE

Infinitive is a grammatical term that refers to the base form of a verb, typically preceded by the word "to." Infinitives are used to express a variety of functions, such as purpose, intention, or possibility. For example, "to run" is the infinitive form of the verb "run." Infinitives can be used as nouns, adjectives, or adverbs, and are often used to express purpose in a sentence. For example, "I came to the store to buy milk" uses the infinitive "to buy" to express the purpose of the subject's trip to the store. Understanding the use of infinitives is crucial for writers, as they can be used to add clarity, express relationships between actions, and create a more sophisticated and nuanced writing style.

Cursive Tips

- Use Pencil to trace Letters

- Learn Basics First

- If you are beginner don't aim for perfection

- Use Ink pens for perfect & elegant Cursive

- Maintain consistent of the style & degree of slants or tilt of words

- Maintain Correct Body posture. Sit up straight & then utilize your non-writing hand for balance

- While writing the words pronounce loudly and read the meaning of respective words which are gives below.

1. *abash*

To make ashamed or uneasy; disconcert.

Present

abash

Example Present

you abash

Past

abashed

Example   Past

you had abashed

Example   Future

you will abash

s / es/ ies

abashes

ing form

abashing

Imperative

let's abash

Infinitive

to abash

2. *abide*

To wait patiently for.

Present

abide

Example Present

you abide

Past

abode

Example Past

you had abode

Example Future

you will abide

s / es/ ies

abides

ing form

abiding

Imperative

let's abide

Infinitive

to abide

3. *abate*

To put an end to.

Present

abate

Example Present

you abate

Past

abated

Example Past

you had abated

Example Future

you will abate

s / es/ ies

abates

ing form

abating

Imperative

let's abate

Infinitive

to abatabide

4. *accept*

To answer affirmatively.

Present

accept

Example Present

you accept

Past

accepted

Example Past

you had accepted

Example Future

you will accept

s / es/ ies

accepts

ing form

accepting

Imperative

let's accept

Infinitive

to accept

5. absorb

To put an end to.

Present

absorb

Example Present

you absorb

Past

absorbed

Example   Past

you had absorbed

Example   Future

you will absorb

s / es/ ies

absorbs

ing form

absorbing

Imperative

let's absorb

Infinitive

to absorb

6. ache

To suffer a dull, sustained pain.

Present

ache

Example Present

you ache

Past

ached

Example Past

you had ached

Example Future

you will ache

s / es/ ies

aches

ing form

aching

Imperative

let's ache

Infinitive

to ache

7. *accompany*

To exist or occur at the same time as.

Present

accompany

Example Present

you accompany

Past

accompanied

Example Past

you had accompanied

Example Future

you will accompany

s / es/ ies

accompanies

ing form

accompanying

Imperative

let's accompany

Infinitive

to accompany

8. *acquire*

To gain possession of.

Present

acquire

Example Present

you acquire

Past

acquired

Example Past

you had acquired

Example Future

you will acquire

s / es/ ies

acquires

ing form

acquiring

Imperative

let's acquire

Infinitive

to acquire

9. achieve

To gain with effort or despite difficulty; reach.

Present

achieve

Example Present

you achieve

Past

achieved

Example Past

you had achieved

Example Future

you will achieve

s / es/ ies

achieves

ing form

achieving

Imperative

let's achieve

Infinitive

to achieve

10. *add*

To say or write further.

Present

add

Example Present

you add

Past

added

Example Past

you had added

Example Future

you will add

s / es/ ies

adds

ing form

adding

Imperative

let's add

Infinitive

to add

11. *act*

Something done or performed; a deed.

Present

act

Example Present

you act

Past

acted

Example Past

you had acted

Example Future

you will act

s / es/ ies

acts

ing form

acting

Imperative

let's act

Infinitive

to act

12. adjust

To change so as to be suitable to or conform with something else

Present

adjust

Example Present

you adjust

Past

adjusted

Example Past

you had adjusted

Example Future

you will adjust

s / es/ ies

adjusts

ing form

adjusting

Imperative

let's adjust

Infinitive

to adjust

13. address

To make a formal speech to.

Present

address

Example Present

you address

Past

addressed

Example Past

you had addressed

Example Future

you will address

s / es/ ies

addresses

ing form

addressing

Imperative

let's address

Infinitive

to address

14. admit

To change so as to be suitable to or conform with something else

Present

admit

Example Present

you admit

Past

admited

Example Past

you had admited

Example Future

you will admit

s / es/ ies

admits

ing form

admiring

Imperative

let's admit

Infinitive

to admit

15. *admire*

To regard with pleasure, wonder, and approval.

Present

admire

Example Present

you admire

Past

admired

Example Past

you had admired

Example Future

you will admire

s / es/ ies

admires

ing form

admiring

Imperative

let's admire

Infinitive

to admire

16. *afford*

To have the financial means for; bear the cost of.

Present

afford

Example Present

you afford

Past

afforded

Example Past

you had afforded

Example Future

you will afford

s / es/ ies

affords

ing form

affording

Imperative

let's afford

Infinitive

to afford

17. *advise*

To offer advice to; counsel.

Present

advise

Example Present

you advise

Past

advised

Example Past

you had advised

Example Future

you will advise

s / es/ ies

advises

ing form

admireing

Imperative

let's advise

Infinitive

to advise

18. *alight*

Provided with light; lighted up; illuminated.

Present

alight

Example Present

you alight

Past

alighted

Example Past

you had alighted

Example Future

you will alight

s / es/ ies

alights

ing form

alighting

Imperative

let's alight

Infinitive

to alight

19. agree

To share an opinion or feeling; be in accord.

Present

agree

Example Present

you agree

Past

agreed

Example Past

you had agreed

Example Future

you will agree

s / es/ ies

agrees

ing form

agreeing

Imperative

let's agree

Infinitive

to agree

20. animate

To give life to; fill with life.

Present

animate

Example Present

you animate

Past

animated

Example Past

you had animated

Example Future

you will animate

s / es/ ies

animates

ing form

animating

Imperative

let's animate

Infinitive

to animate

21. *allow*

To permit to have.

Present

allow

Example Present

you allow

Past

allowed

Example Past

you had allowd

Example Future

you will allow

s / es/ ies

allows

ing form

allowing

Imperative

let's allow

Infinitive

to allow

22. answer

A spoken or written reply, as to a question.

Present

answer

Example Present

you answer

Past

answered

Example Past

you had answered

Example Future

you will answer

s / es/ ies

answers

ing form

answering

Imperative

let's answer

Infinitive

to answer

23. *announce*

To make known publicly.

Present

announce

Example Present

you announce

Past

announced

Example Past

you had announced

Example Future

you will announce

s / es/ ies

announces

ing form

announcing

Imperative

let's announce

Infinitive

to announce

24. *appear*

To become visible.

Present

appear

Example Present

you appear

Past

appeared

Example Past

you had appeared

Example Future

you will appear

s / es/ ies

appears

ing form

appearing

Imperative

let's appear

Infinitive

to appear

25. *apologize*

To make a formal defense or justification in speech or writing.

Present

apologize

Example Present

you apologize

Past

apologized

Example Past

you had apologized

Example Future

you will apologize

s / es/ ies

apologizes

ing form

apologizing

Imperative

let's apologize

Infinitive

to apologize

26. *apply*

To put into action.

Present

apply

Example Present

you apply

Past

applyed

Example Past

you had applyed

Example Future

you will apply

s / es/ ies

applies

ing form

applying

Imperative

let's apply

Infinitive

to apply

27. *applaud*

To express approval, especially by clapping the hands.

Present

applaud

Example Present

you applaud

Past

applauded

Example Past

you had applauded

Example Future

you will applaud

s / es/ ies

applauds

ing form

applauding

Imperative

let's applaud

Infinitive

to applaud

28. approve

To prove or attest.

Present

approve

Example Present

you approve

Past

approved

Example Past

you had approved

Example Future

you will approve

s / es/ ies

approves

ing form

approving

Imperative

let's approve

Infinitive

to approve

29. *approach*

To come or go near or nearer to.

Present

approach

Example Present

you approach

Past

approached

Example Past

you had approached

Example Future

you will approach

s / es/ ies

approaches

ing form

approaching

Imperative

let's approach

Infinitive

to approach

30. arise

To move upward; ascend.

Present

arise

Example Present

you arise

Past

arised

Example Past

you had arisen

Example Future

you will arise

s / es/ ies

arises

ing form

arising

Imperative

let's arise

Infinitive

to arise

31. *argue*

To put forth reasons for or against; debate.

Present

argue

Example Present

you argue

Past

argued

Example Past

you had argued

Example Future

you will argue

s / es/ ies

argues

ing form

arguing

Imperative

let's argue

Infinitive

to argue

32. *arrest*

To stop; check.

Present

arrest

Example Present

you arrest

Past

arrested

Example   Past

you had arrested

Example   Future

you will arrest

s / es/ ies

arrests

ing form

arresting

Imperative

let's arrest

Infinitive

to arrest

33. *arrange*

To plan or prepare for.

Present

arrange

Example Present

you arrange

Past

arranged

Example Past

you had arranged

Example Future

you will arrange

s / es/ ies

arranges

ing form

arranging

Imperative

let's arrange

Infinitive

to arrange

34. *assert*

To state or express positively; affirm.

Present

assert

Example Present

you assert

Past

asserted

Example Past

you had asserted

Example Future

you will assert

s / es / ies

asserts

ing form

asserting

Imperative

let's assert

Infinitive

to assert

35. ask

To put a question to.

Present

ask

Example Present

you ask

Past

asked

Example Past

you had asked

Example Future

you will ask

s / es / ies

asks

ing form

asking

Imperative

let's ask

Infinitive

to ask

36. astonish

To fill with sudden wonder or amazement. synonym: surprise.

Present

astonish

Example Present

you astonish

Past

astonished

Example Past

you had astonished

Example Future

you will astonish

s / es/ ies

astonishes

ing form

astonishing

Imperative

let's astonish

Infinitive

to astonish

37. *assort*

To agree in kind; fall into the same class.

Present

assort

Example Present

you assort

Past

assorted

Example Past

you had assorted

Example Future

you will assort

s / es/ ies

assorts

ing form

assorting

Imperative

let's assort

Infinitive

to assort

38. attend

To be present at.

Present

attend

Example Present

you attend

Past

attended

Example Past

you had attended

Example Future

you will attend

s / es/ ies

attends

ing form

attending

Imperative

let's attend

Infinitive

to attend

39. attack

To set upon with violent force.

Present

attack

Example Present

you attack

Past

attacked

Example   Past

you had attacked

Example   Future

you will attack

s / es/ ies

attacks

ing form

attacking

Imperative

let's attack

Infinitive

to attack

40. *audit*

An examined and verified account.

Present

audit

Example Present

you audit

Past

audited

Example Past

you had audited

Example Future

you will audit

s / es/ ies

audits

ing form

auditing

Imperative

let's audit

Infinitive

to audit

41. attract

To cause to draw near or adhere by physical force.

Present

attract

Example Present

you attract

Past

attracted

Example Past

you had attracted

Example Future

you will attract

s / es/ ies

attracts

ing form

attracting

Imperative

let's attract

Infinitive

to attract

42. *awake*

To rouse from sleep; waken.

Present

awake

Example Present

you awake

Past

awoken

Example Past

you had awoken

Example Future

you will awake

s / es/ ies

awakes

ing form

awaking

Imperative

let's awake

Infinitive

to awake

43. *avoid*

To stay clear of; go around or away from.

Present

avoid

Example Present

you avoid

Past

avoided

Example Past

you had avoided

Example Future

you will avoid

s / es/ ies

avoids

ing form

avoiding

Imperative

let's avoid

Infinitive

to avoid

44. banish

To drive away; expel.

Present

banish

Example Present

you banish

Past

banished

Example Past

you had banished

Example Future

you will banish

s / es/ ies

banishes

ing form

banishing

Imperative

let's banish

Infinitive

to banish

45. bang
A sudden burst of action.

Present
bang

Example Present
you bang

Past
banged

Example Past
you had banged

Example Future
you will bang

s / es/ ies
bangs

ing form
banging

Imperative
let's bang

Infinitive
to bang

46. *bat*

To hit with or as if with a bat.

Present

bat

Example Present

you bat

Past

batted

Example Past

you had batted

Example Future

you will bat

s / es / ies

bats

ing form

bating

Imperative

let's bat

Infinitive

to bat

47. bash

To strike with a heavy, crushing blow.

Present

bash

Example Present

you bash

Past

bashed

Example Past

you had bashed

Example Future

you will bash

s / es/ ies

bashs

ing form

bashing

Imperative

let's bash

Infinitive

to bash

48. *bear*

To cause to move by or with steady pressure; push.

Present

bear

Example Present

you bear

Past

borne

Example Past

you had borne

Example Future

you will bear

s / es/ ies

bears

ing form

bearing

Imperative

let's bear

Infinitive

to bear

49. be

Exist / occur ; take place

Present

be

Example Present

you are

Past

been

Example Past

you had been

Example Future

you will be

s / es/ ies

is

ing form

being

Imperative

let's be

Infinitive

to be

50. beat

To strike repeatedly.

Present

beat

Example Present

you beat

Past

beaten

Example Past

you had beaten

Example Future

you will beat

s / es/ ies

beats

ing form

beating

Imperative

let's beat

Infinitive

to beat

51. *beautify*

To make or become beautiful.

Present

beautify

Example Present

you beautify

Past

beautified

Example Past

you had beautified

Example Future

you will beautify

s / es/ ies

beautifies

ing form

beautifying

Imperative

let's beautify

Infinitive

to beautify

52. *befall*

To come to pass; happen.

Present

befall

Example Present

you befall

Past

befallen

Example Past

you had befallen

Example Future

you will befall

s / es/ ies

befalls

ing form

befalling

Imperative

let's befall

Infinitive

to befall

53. become

To grow or come to be.

Present

become

Example Present

you become

Past

became

Example Past

you had became

Example Future

you will become

s / es/ ies

becomes

ing form

becoming

Imperative

let's become

Infinitive

to become

54. *begin*

To perform or undergo the first part of an action; start.

Present

begin

Example Present

you begin

Past

begin

Example Past

you had begun

Example Future

you will begin

s / es/ ies

begins

ing form

beginning

Imperative

let's begin

Infinitive

to begin

55. beg

To ask for (something) in an urgent or humble manner.

Present

beg

Example Present

you beg

Past

begged

Example Past

you had begged

Example Future

you will beg

s / es/ ies

begs

ing form

begging

Imperative

let's beg

Infinitive

to beg

56. behold

To see, look upon, or gaze at

Present

behold

Example Present

you behold

Past

beheld

Example Past

you had beheld

Example Future

you will behold

s / es/ ies

beholds

ing form

beholding

Imperative

let's behold

Infinitive

to behold

57. behave

To conduct oneself in a proper way.

Present

behave

Example Present

you behave

Past

behaved

Example Past

you had behaved

Example Future

you will behave

s / es/ ies

behaves

ing form

behaving

Imperative

let's behave

Infinitive

to behave

58. belong

To be proper, appropriate, or suitable.

Present

belong

Example Present

you belong

Past

belonged

Example Past

you had belonged

Example Future

you will belong

s / es/ ies

belongs

ing form

belonging

Imperative

let's belong

Infinitive

to belong

59. believe

To accept as true or real.

Present

believe

Example Present

you believe

Past

believed

Example Past

you had believed

Example Future

you will believe

s / es/ ies

believes

ing form

believing

Imperative

let's believe

Infinitive

to believe

60. *bereave*

To take a loved one from (a person), especially by death.

Present

bereave

Example Present

you bereave

Past

bereaft

Example Past

you had bereaft

Example Future

you will bereave

s / es/ ies

bereaves

ing form

bereaving

Imperative

let's bereave

Infinitive

to bereave

61. bend

A knot that joins a rope to a rope or another object.

Present

bend

Example Present

you bend

Past

bent

Example Past

you had bent

Example Future

you will bend

s / es/ ies

bends

ing form

bending

Imperative

let's bend

Infinitive

to bend

62. bet

An amount or object risked in a wager; a stake.

Present

bet

Example Present

you bet

Past

beted

Example Past

you had beted

Example Future

you will bet

s / es/ ies

bets

ing form

betting

Imperative

let's bet

Infinitive

to bet

63. beseech

To request earnestly; beg for.

Present

beseech

Example Present

you beseech

Past

besought

Example Past

you had besought

Example Future

you will beseech

s / es/ ies

beseeches

ing form

beseeching

Imperative

let's beseech

Infinitive

to beseech

64. bid

To offer or propose (an amount) as a price.

Present

bid

Example Present

you bid

Past

bid

Example Past

you had bid

Example Future

you will bid

s / es/ ies

bids

ing form

bidding

Imperative

let's bid

Infinitive

to bid

65. betray

To be false or disloyal to.

Present

betray

Example Present

you betray

Past

betrayed

Example Past

you had betrayed

Example Future

you will betray

s / es/ ies

betrays

ing form

betraying

Imperative

let's betray

Infinitive

to betray

66. bite

To cut, grip, or tear with or as if with the teeth.

Present

bite

Example Present

you bite

Past

bitten

Example Past

you had bitten

Example Future

you will bite

s / es/ ies

bites

ing form

biting

Imperative

let's bite

Infinitive

to bite

67. bind

To tie or secure, as with a rope or cord.

Present

bind

Example Present

you bind

Past

bindd

Example Past

you had bindd

Example Future

you will bind

s / es / ies

binds

ing form

binding

Imperative

let's bind

Infinitive

to bind

68. *bless*

To make holy by religious rite; sanctify.

Present

bless

Example Present

you bless

Past

blessed

Example Past

you had blessed

Example Future

you will bless

s / es / ies

blesses

ing form

blessing

Imperative

let's bless

Infinitive

to bless

69. bleed

To emit or lose blood.

Present

bleed

Example Present

you bleed

Past

bled

Example Past

you had bled

Example Future

you will bleed

s / es/ ies

bleeds

ing form

bleeding

Imperative

let's bleed

Infinitive

to bleed

70. *blow*

To bloom or cause to bloom.

Present

blow

Example Present

you blow

Past

blown

Example Past

you had blown

Example Future

you will blow

s / es/ ies

blows

ing form

blowing

Imperative

let's blow

Infinitive

to blow

71. *blossom*

To come into flower; bloom.

Present

blossom

Example Present

you blossom

Past

blossomed

Example Past

you had blossomed

Example Future

you will blossom

s / es/ ies

blossoms

ing form

blossoming

Imperative

let's blossom

Infinitive

to blossom

72. blush

To become red or rosy.

Present

blush

Example Present

you blush

Past

blushed

Example Past

you had blushed

Example Future

you will blush

s / es/ ies

blushes

ing form

blushing

Imperative

let's blush

Infinitive

to blush

73. blur

To make dim, unclear, or cloudy.

Present

blur

Example Present

you blur

Past

blurred

Example Past

you had blurred

Example Future

you will blur

s / es/ ies

blurs

ing form

blurring

Imperative

let's blur

Infinitive

to blur

74. boast

To shape or form (stone) roughly with a broad chisel.

Present

boast

Example Present

you boast

Past

boasted

Example Past

you had boasted

Example Future

you will boast

s / es/ ies

boasts

ing form

boasting

Imperative

let's boast

Infinitive

to boast

75. board

A long flat slab of sawed lumber; a plank.

Present

board

Example Present

you board

Past

boardd

Example Past

you had boardd

Example Future

you will board

s / es/ ies

boards

ing form

boarding

Imperative

let's board

Infinitive

to board

76. *bow*

To bend or curve downward; stoop.

Present

bow

Example Present

you bow

Past

bowed

Example Past

you had bowed

Example Future

you will bow

s / es/ ies

bows

ing form

bowing

Imperative

let's bow

Infinitive

to bow

77. *boil*

To reach the boiling point.

Present

boil

Example Present

you boil

Past

boiled

Example Past

you had boiled

Example Future

you will boil

s / es/ ies

boils

ing form

boiling

Imperative

let's boil

Infinitive

to boil

78. bray

To crush and pound to a fine consistency, as in a mortar.

Present

bray

Example Present

you bray

Past

brayed

Example Past

you had brayed

Example Future

you will bray

s / es/ ies

brays

ing form

braying

Imperative

let's bray

Infinitive

to bray

79. box

The amount or quantity that such a container can hold.

Present

box

Example Present

you box

Past

boxed

Example Past

you had boxed

Example Future

you will box

s / es/ ies

boxes

ing form

boxing

Imperative

let's box

Infinitive

to box

80. *breathe*

To inhale and exhale air using the lungs.

Present

breathe

Example Present

you breathe

Past

breathed

Example Past

you had breathed

Example Future

you will breathe

s / es/ ies

breathes

ing form

breatheing

Imperative

let's breathe

Infinitive

to breathe

81. break

To cause to separate into pieces suddenly or violently; smash.

Present

break

Example Present

you break

Past

broken

Example Past

you had broken

Example Future

you will break

s / es / ies

breaks

ing form

breaking

Imperative

let's break

Infinitive

to break

82. bring

To carry, convey, lead, or cause to go along to another place.

Present

bring

Example Present

you bring

Past

brought

Example Past

you had brought

Example Future

you will bring

s / es/ ies

brings

ing form

bringing

Imperative

let's bring

Infinitive

to bring

83. *breed*

To produce (offspring); give birth to or hatch.

Present

breed

Example Present

you breed

Past

bred

Example Past

you had bred

Example Future

you will breed

s / es/ ies

breeds

ing form

breeding

Imperative

let's breed

Infinitive

to breed

84. brush

The act of using this implement.

Present

brush

Example Present

you brush

Past

brushed

Example Past

you had brushed

Example Future

you will brush

s / es/ ies

brushes

ing form

brushing

Imperative

let's brush

Infinitive

to brush

85. *broadcast*

To sow (seed) over a wide area, especially by hand.

Present

broadcast

Example Present

you broadcast

Past

broadcast

Example Past

you had broadcast

Example Future

you will broadcast

s / es/ ies

broadcasts

ing form

broadcasting

Imperative

let's broadcast

Infinitive

to broadcast

86. burn

To undergo combustion also to undergo nuclear fission or nuclear fusion.

Present

burn

Example Present

you burn

Past

burnt

Example Past

you had burnt

Example Future

you will burn

s / es/ ies

burns

ing form

burning

Imperative

let's burn

Infinitive

to burn

87. build

To form by combining materials or parts; construct.

Present

build

Example Present

you build

Past

built

Example Past

you had built

Example Future

you will build

s / es/ ies

builds

ing form

building

Imperative

let's build

Infinitive

to build

88. *bury*

To place in the ground; cover with earth.

Present

bury

Example Present

you bury

Past

buried

Example Past

you had buried

Example Future

you will bury

s / es/ ies

buries

ing form

burying

Imperative

let's bury

Infinitive

to bury

89. *burst*

To explode.

Present

burst

Example Present

you burst

Past

bursted

Example Past

you had bursted

Example Future

you will burst

s / es/ ies

bursts

ing form

bursting

Imperative

let's burst

Infinitive

to burst

90. buy

To acquire by sacrifice, exchange, or trade.

Present

buy

Example Present

you buy

Past

bought

Example Past

you had bought

Example Future

you will buy

s / es/ ies

buys

ing form

buying

Imperative

let's buy

Infinitive

to buy

91. *bust*

To smash or break, especially forcefully.

Present

bust

Example Present

you bust

Past

bustd

Example Past

you had bustd

Example Future

you will bust

s / es/ ies

busts

ing form

busting

Imperative

let's bust

Infinitive

to bust

92. calculate

To ascertain by computation; reckon.

Present

calculate

Example Present

you calculate

Past

calculated

Example Past

you had calculated

Example Future

you will calculate

s / es/ ies

calculates

ing form

calculating

Imperative

let's calculate

Infinitive

to calculate

93. *buzz*

To talk, often excitedly, in low tones.

Present

buzz

Example Present

you buzz

Past

buzzed

Example Past

you had buzzed

Example Future

you will buzz

s / es/ ies

buzzes

ing form

buzzing

Imperative

let's buzz

Infinitive

to buzz

94. *canvass*

To examine carefully or discuss thoroughly; scrutinize.

Present

canvass

Example Present

you canvass

Past

canvassed

Example   Past

you had canvassed

Example   Future

you will canvass

s / es/ ies

canvass

ing form

canvassing

Imperative

let's canvass

Infinitive

to canvass

95. call

To say in a loud voice; announce.

Present

call

Example Present

you call

Past

called

Example Past

you had called

Example Future

you will call

s / es/ ies

calls

ing form

calling

Imperative

let's call

Infinitive

to call

96. *caress*

To touch or stroke in an affectionate or loving manner.

Present

caress

Example Present

you caress

Past

caressed

Example Past

you had caressed

Example Future

you will caress

s / es/ ies

caresses

ing form

caressing

Imperative

let's caress

Infinitive

to caress

97. *capture*

To take captive, as by force or craft; seize.

Present

capture

Example Present

you capture

Past

captured

Example Past

you had captured

Example Future

you will capture

s / es/ ies

captures

ing form

captureing

Imperative

let's capture

Infinitive

to capture

98. carve

To divide into pieces by cutting; slice.

Present

carve

Example Present

you carve

Past

carved

Example Past

you had carved

Example Future

you will carve

s / es/ ies

carves

ing form

carving

Imperative

let's carve

Infinitive

to carve

99. carry

To hold or support while moving; bear.

Present

carry

Example Present

you carry

Past

carried

Example Past

you had carried

Example Future

you will carry

s / es / ies

carries

ing form

carrying

Imperative

let's carry

Infinitive

to carry

100 cast

To throw (something, especially something light).

Present

cast

Example Present

you cast

Past

cast

Example Past

you had cast

Example Future

you will cast

s / es/ ies

casts

ing form

casting

Imperative

let's cast

Infinitive

to cast

101. cash

To exchange for or convert into ready money.

Present

cash

Example Present

you cash

Past

cast

Example Past

you had cast

Example Future

you will cash

s / es/ ies

cashes

ing form

cashing

Imperative

let's cash

Infinitive

to cash

102. cause

The producer of an effect, result, or consequence.

Present

cause

Example Present

you cause

Past

caused

Example Past

you had caused

Example Future

you will cause

s / es/ ies

causes

ing form

causing

Imperative

let's cause

Infinitive

to cause

Made in United States
Troutdale, OR
05/18/2025

31442381R00064